Icelandic Word of the Day:

365 High Frequency Words to Accelerate Your Icelandic Vocabulary

ISBN: 1532881339
ISBN–13: 978-1532881336

CONTENTS

INTRODUCTION

Learning a new language involves learning a lot of new vocabulary. Although the grammar and pronunciation of a language can seem like the most difficult parts, especially a difficult language like Icelandic, the real challenge quickly becomes learning the thousands of new words you require to speak a new language fluently.

How to find the right words and how to efficiently memorize them are the problems that many language learners face near the beginning of their studies. The goal of this book is to fill the gap by providing you with a new, high frequency Icelandic word to learn every day. At the end of the year (or much sooner) you will be 365 words closer to your goal of speaking Icelandic.

Did you know that in English, the most common 100 words make up nearly half of every sentence, and that other languages have similar frequency distributions? This is a powerful concept that is underused in many language courses. By focusing on the high frequency words, this book will accelerate your Icelandic vocabulary more efficiently than merely learning the random lists of words that learners sometimes face, and by providing the words to you, this book will save you from the time-consuming process of searching for all those new words yourself.

The outline of this book is a new word every day for a year. In this way you can be sure that you are making progress even on days where you don't have time to study. Carry this word around with you and review it throughout

i

the day. Of course many people will progress faster through this book and will want more than one word a day and in that case the reader should go at whatever pace feels comfortable. I would still encourage you go back to the word of the day to review on that specific day, just to ensure that you have thoroughly learned it. Remember repetition is the mother of all learning.

Good luck on your language learning journey and I hope you enjoy your Icelandic Word of the Day!

ICELANDIC ALPHABET AND PRONUNCIATION

The Icelandic language uses the same Latin alphabet as English with some additional letters, some of which are used only in Icelandic. The complete Icelandic alphabet, with a simple pronunciation guide to each letter, is shown below:

Letter	Pronunciation
Aa	"a" as in tar
Áá	"ou" as in house
Bb	"p" as in spit
Dd	"t" as in stare
Ðð	"th" as in father
Ee	"e" as in bed
Éé	"ye" as in yes
Ff	"f" as in far
Gg	"g" as in good at the beginning of a word; "y" in "yes" between vowel and –i or –j; silent between á, ó, ú, and a or u
Hh	"h" as in happy
Ii	"i" as in bit
Íí	"ee" as in bee
Jj	"y" as in yes
Kk	"k" as in kick
Ll	"l" as in love
Mm	"m" as in mother
Nn	"n" as in new
Oo	"o" as in cot

Óó	"o" as in hope
Pp	"p" as in peer
Rr	rolled or trilled "r" as in Spanish
Ss	"s" as in same
Tt	"t" as in tea
Uu	similar to the "u" in cute; same as the French u or the German ü
Úú	"oo" as in food
Vv	between an English "v" and a "w"
Xx	"x" as in six
Yy	same as Icelandic i
Ýý	same as Icelandic í
Þþ	"th" in thunder, same as ð above
Ææ	"igh" as in high
Öö	"ir" as in thirst; same as the German ö

Icelandic can be a difficult language to pronounce for an English speaker, although the written word usually matches the pronunciation pretty well once you get used to the Icelandic spelling and the new letters. If you are unsure about the pronunciation, I recommend going to forvo.com and typing in the Icelandic word to hear a native speaker pronounce it.

There are three noun genders in Icelandic, masculine, feminine and neuter. The gender of the noun is important to know, as the noun and adjective forms are affected by the noun's gender. The gender is given below each noun in this book so that it can be learned along with the word on that day.

Jan. 1

stríð

war (neuter)

Jan. 2

morgunmatur

breakfast (masculine)

Jan. 3

bátur

boat (masculine)

Jan. 4

ár

year (neuter)

Jan. 5

móðir

mother (feminine)

Jan. 6

hnífur

knife (masculine)

Jan. 7

elska

to love

Jan. 8

úlfur

wolf (masculine)

Jan. 9

veikur

sick

Jan. 10

bar

bar (place to drink) (masculine)

Jan. 11

hægur

slow

Jan. 12

dýr

expensive

Jan. 13

kvöldmatur

dinner (masculine)

Jan. 14

einfaldur

easy

Jan. 15

hár

hair (neuter)

Jan. 16

vandamál

problem (neuter)

Jan. 17

egg

egg (neuter)

Jan. 18

jakki

coat (masculine)

Jan. 19

smá

a little

Jan. 20

hattur

hat (masculine)

Jan. 21

stór

big

Jan. 22

helmingur

half (masculine)

Jan. 23

ganga

to walk

Jan. 24

veikur

weak

Jan. 25

mús

mouse (feminine)

Jan. 26

samur

same

Jan. 27

lögfræðingur

lawyer (masculine)

Jan. 28

sterkur

strong

Jan. 29

muna

to remember

Jan. 30

skeið

spoon (feminine)

Jan. 31

hamingjusamur

happy

Feb. 1

draga

to pull

Feb. 2

hermaður

soldier (masculine)

Feb. 3

gras

grass (neuter)

Feb. 4

kjúklingur

chicken (masculine)

Feb. 5

málmur

metal (masculine)

Feb. 6

falla

to fall

Feb. 7

nótt

night (feminine)

Feb. 8

votur

wet

Feb. 9

slá

to hit

Feb. 10

lauf

leaf (neuter)

Feb. 11

sjá

to see

Feb. 12

amma

grandmother (feminine)

Feb. 13

banani

banana (masculine)

Feb. 14

leika

to play

Feb. 15

syngja

to sing

Feb. 16

tré

tree (neuter)

Feb. 17

dansa

to dance

Feb. 18

eiginkona

wife (feminine)

Feb. 19

vísindi

science (neuter)

Feb. 20

kirsuber

cherry (neuter)

Feb. 21

snemma

early

Feb. 22

mánuður

month (masculine)

Feb. 23

læra

to learn

Feb. 24

verslun

store / shop (feminine)

Mar. 13

selja

to sell

Mar. 14

morgunn

morning (masculine)

Mar. 15

sokkur

sock (masculine)

Mar. 16

hlæja

to laugh

Mar. 17

kýr

cow (feminine)

Mar. 18

ávöxtur

fruit (masculine)

Mar. 19

hljóður

quiet

Mar. 20

í gær

yesterday

Mar. 21

heili

brain (masculine)

Mar. 22

fljót

river (neuter)

Mar. 23

dýr

animal (neuter)

Mar. 24

hús

house (neuter)

Mar. 25

vasi

pocket (masculine)

Mar. 26

friður

peace (masculine)

Mar. 27

blóm

flower (neuter)

Mar. 28

skera

to cut

Mar. 29

stúlka

girl (feminine)

Mar. 30

vakna

to wake up

Mar. 31

loft

air (neuter)

Apr. 1

vör

lip (feminine)

Apr. 2

tá

toe (feminine)

Apr. 3

norður

north (neuter)

Apr. 4

ólíkur

different

Apr. 5

elda

to cook

Apr. 6

eldur

fire (masculine)

Apr. 7

kaka

cake (feminine)

Apr. 8

regnhlíf

umbrella (feminine)

Apr. 9

klæðnaður

clothing (masculine)

Apr. 10

borð

table (neuter)

Apr. 11

sjúkrahús

hospital (neuter)

Apr. 12

grípa

to catch

Apr. 13

kennari

teacher (masculine)

Apr. 14

hótel

hotel (neuter)

Apr. 15

nafn

name (neuter)

Apr. 16

mjólk

milk (feminine)

Apr. 17

tönn

tooth (feminine)

Apr. 18

veggur

wall (masculine)

Apr. 19

farmiði

ticket (masculine)

Apr. 20

alltaf

always

Apr. 21

stöð

train station (feminine)

Apr. 22

mál

language (neuter)

Apr. 23

fingur

finger (masculine)

Apr. 24

ey

island (feminine)

Apr. 25

fótur

leg (masculine)

Apr. 26

karlmaður

man (masculine)

Apr. 27

ýta

to push

Apr. 28

finna

to find

Apr. 29

bók

book (feminine)

Apr. 30

salt

salt (neuter)

May 1

gólf

floor (neuter)

May 2

lamb

lamb (neuter)

May 3

kaffi

coffee (neuter)

May 4

tómatur

tomato (feminine)

May 21

þykkur

thick

May 22

kasta

to throw

May 23

langur

long

May 24

sól

sun (masculine)

May 25

tunga

tongue (feminine)

May 26

kaldur

cold

May 27

blár

blue

May 28

hugmynd

idea (feminine)

May 29

lykill

key (masculine)

May 30

aka

to drive

May 31

óhreinn

dirty

Jun. 1

kaupa

to buy

Jun. 2

íþrótt

sport (feminine)

Jun. 3

háls

neck (masculine)

Jun. 4

slást

to fight

Jun. 5

hádegismatur

lunch (masculine)

Jun. 6

fjall

mountain (neuter)

Jun. 7

snjór

snow (masculine)

Jun. 8

nautakjöt

beef (neuter)

Jun. 9

skór

shoe (masculine)

Jun. 10

hver

who

Jun. 11

þorp

village (neuter)

Jun. 12

grænmeti

vegetable (neuter)

Jun. 13

stjarna

star (feminine)

Jun. 14

penni

pen (masculine)

Jun. 15

vín

wine (neuter)

Jun. 16

vilja

to want

Jun. 17

vinna

to work

Jun. 18

hjarta

heart (neuter)

Jun. 19

lesa

to read

Jun. 20

lyklaborð

keyboard (neuter)

Jun. 21

manneskja

human (feminine)

Jun. 22

þröngur

narrow

Jun. 23

þak

roof (neuter)

Jun. 24

flaska

bottle (feminine)

Jun. 25

hundur

dog (masculine)

Jun. 26

bíll

car (masculine)

Jun. 27

auga

eye (neuter)

Jun. 28

hjálpa

to help

Jun. 29

skóli

school (masculine)

Jun. 30

skegg

beard (neuter)

Jul. 1

vetur

winter (masculine)

Jul. 2

vestur

west (neuter)

Jul. 3

ljós

light (neuter)

Jul. 4

líkami

body (masculine)

Jul. 5

dóttir

daughter (feminine)

Jul. 6

sviti

sweat (masculine)

Jul. 7

orðabók

dictionary (feminine)

Jul. 8

smár

small

Jul. 9

vopn

weapon (neuter)

Jul. 10

synda

to swim

Jul. 11

vinna

to win

Jul. 12

ríkur

rich

Jul. 13

bróðir

brother (masculine)

Jul. 14

tungl

moon (neuter)

Jul. 15

björn

bear (masculine)

Jul. 16

vinur

friend (masculine)

Jul. 17

heitur

hot

Jul. 18

vindur

wind (masculine)

Jul. 19

park

park (masculine)

Jul. 20

þurr

dry

Jul. 21

blóð

blood (neuter)

Jul. 22

regn

rain (neuter)

Jul. 23

í dag

today

Jul. 24

reipi

rope (neuter)

Jul. 25

stígvél

boot (neuter)

Jul. 26

dagblað

newspaper (neuter)

Jul. 27

sjónvarp

television (neuter)

Jul. 28

leðja

mud (feminine)

Jul. 29

höfuð

head (neuter)

Jul. 30

steinn

stone (masculine)

Jul. 31

þegar

already

Aug. 1

grænn

green

Aug. 2

diskur

plate (masculine)

Aug. 3

draumur

dream (masculine)

Aug. 4

hreinn

clean

Aug. 5

veski

wallet (neuter)

Aug. 6

ljótur

ugly

Aug. 7

tónlist

music (feminine)

Aug. 8

drepa

to kill

Aug. 9

svín

pig (neuter)

Aug. 10

ekkert

nothing

Aug. 11

hestur

horse (masculine)

Aug. 12

haf

sea (neuter)

Aug. 13

bjór

beer (masculine)

Aug. 14

læknir

doctor (masculine)

Aug. 15

appelsínugulur

orange (color)

Aug. 16

nemandi

student (masculine)

Aug. 17

borga

to pay

Aug. 18

austur

east (neuter)

Aug. 19

lögregla

police (feminine)

Aug. 20

nú

now

Aug. 21

lest

train (feminine)

Aug. 22

brú

bridge (feminine)

Aug. 23

köttur

cat (masculine)

Aug. 24

tapa

to lose

Aug. 25

kort

map (neuter)

Aug. 26

vika

week (feminine)

Aug. 27

dapur

sad

Aug. 28

súpa

soup (feminine)

Aug. 29

dyr

door (feminine)

Aug. 30

framtíð

future (feminine)

Aug. 31

epli

apple (neuter)

Sep. 1

á morgun

tomorrow

Sep. 2

illur

evil

Sep. 3

drekka

to drink

Sep. 4

athyglisverður

interesting

Sep. 5

margur

many

Sep. 6

stuttur

short

Sep. 7

strætisvagn

bus (masculine)

Sep. 8

vona

to hope

Sep. 9

hægri

right

Sep. 10

garður

garden (masculine)

Sep. 11

gleyma

to forget

Sep. 12

fugl

bird (masculine)

Sep. 13

haust

autumn (neuter)

Sep. 14

fjölskylda

family (feminine)

Sep. 15

hvað

what

Sep. 16

svefnherbergi

bedroom (neuter)

Sep. 17

poki

bag (masculine)

Sep. 18

kyssa

to kiss

Sep. 19

salerni

bathroom (neuter)

Sep. 20

húð

skin (feminine)

Sep. 21

klukkustund

hour (feminine)

Sep. 22

þunnur

thin

Sep. 23

fylgja

to follow

Sep. 24

appelsína

orange (fruit) (feminine)

Sep. 25

fundur

meeting (masculine)

Sep. 26

leikur

game (masculine)

Sep. 27

vor

spring (neuter)

Sep. 28

deyja

to die

Sep. 29

nef

nose (neuter)

Sep. 30

rúm

bed (neuter)

Oct. 1

pils

skirt (neuter)

Oct. 2

kirkja

church (feminine)

Oct. 3

buxur

pants (plural)

Oct. 4

hlaupa

to run

Oct. 5

myndavél

camera (feminine)

Oct. 6

herbergi

room (neuter)

Oct. 7

sofa

to sleep

Oct. 8

handleggur

arm (masculine)

Oct. 9

vita

to know

Oct. 10

klifra

to climb

Oct. 11

rafhlaða

battery (feminine)

Oct. 12

loka

to close

Oct. 13

hvenær

when

Oct. 14

kona

woman (feminine)

Oct. 15

smjör

butter (neuter)

Oct. 16

gulur

yellow

Oct. 17

safi

juice (masculine)

Oct. 18

land

country (neuter)

Oct. 19

hoppa

to jump

Oct. 20

strákur

boy (masculine)

Oct. 21

girðing

fence (feminine)

Oct. 22

faðir

father (masculine)

Oct. 23

salat

salad (neuter)

Oct. 24

mínúta

minute (feminine)

Oct. 25

byggja

to build

Oct. 26

eyra

ear (neuter)

Oct. 27

saga

story (feminine)

Oct. 28

leiðinlegur

boring

Oct. 29

te

tea (masculine)

Oct. 30

einhver

somebody

Oct. 31

kannski

maybe

Nov. 1

bolli

cup

Nov. 2

skrifstofa

office (feminine)

Nov. 3

kjóll

dress (masculine)

Nov. 4

lyf

medicine (neuter)

Nov. 5

píla

arrow (feminine)

Nov. 6

peningur

money (masculine)

Nov. 7

mikilvægur

important

Nov. 8

opna

to open

Nov. 9

pipar

pepper (masculine)

Nov. 10

svartur

black

Nov. 11

gera

to make

Nov. 12

svínakjöt

pork (neuter)

Nov. 13

skinka

ham (feminine)

Nov. 14

ljúga

to tell a lie

Nov. 15

gráta

to cry

Nov. 16

borða

to eat

Nov. 17

víður

wide

Nov. 18

þvo

to wash

Nov. 19

sitja

to sit

Nov. 20

seint

late

Nov. 21

gifting

wedding (feminine)

Nov. 22

gulrót

carrot (feminine)

Nov. 23

rödd

voice (feminine)

Nov. 24

blýantur

pencil (masculine)

Nov. 25

lykta

to smell

Nov. 26

hvítur

white

Nov. 27

menning

culture (feminine)

Nov. 28

andlit

face (neuter)

Nov. 29

suður

south (neuter)

Nov. 30

veitingastaður

restaurant (masculine)

Dec. 1

hve

how

Dec. 2

dauður

dead

Dec. 3

reiðhjól

bicycle (neuter)

Dec. 4

fljótur

fast

Dec. 5

skógur

forest (masculine)

Dec. 6

flugvöllur

airport (masculine)

Dec. 7

sekúnda

second (feminine)

Dec. 8

dagur

day (masculine)

Dec. 9

bær

farm (masculine)

Dec. 10

grænmetisæta

vegetarian (feminine)

Dec. 11

vínber

grape (neuter)

Dec. 12

fiskur

fish (masculine)

Dec. 13

list

art (feminine)

Dec. 14

erfiður

difficult

Dec. 15

olía

oil (cooking) (feminine)

Dec. 16

safn

museum (neuter)

Dec. 17

brosa

to smile

Dec. 18

fallegur

beautiful

Dec. 19

lifandi

alive

Dec. 20

tölva

computer (feminine)

Dec. 21

munnur

mouth (masculine)

Dec. 22

hlusta

to listen

Dec. 23

eitthvað

something

Dec. 24

fátækur

poor

Dec. 25

parkera

to park

Dec. 26

fljúga

to fly

Dec. 27

vatn

water (neuter)

Dec. 28

skál

bowl (feminine)

Dec. 29

þar sem

where

Dec. 30

skrifa

to write

Dec. 31

klukka

clock (feminine)

Made in the USA
Las Vegas, NV
09 July 2023

74420685R00059